THE ESSENTIAL ALKALINE RECIPES FOR BEGINNERS

Set Yourself on a Path to Optimal Health, The Key to a Longer Life with 25+ Tempting Recipes for Beginners.

BY

Warwick Doyle

Table of Contents

INTRODUCTION

Here are 4 Life-Changing Benefits of Following an Alkaline Diet:

Battles against Fatigue: Too much corrosive in the body diminishes the stockpile of oxygen. This declines the cell's capacity fix and gather supplements. On the off chance that you feel lethargic and tired for the duration of the day, even with the appropriate measure of rest, this could be the pointless development of corrosive.

Reinforces Immune System: Unbalance in pH lessens the body's capacity to battle microscopic organisms and infections. Without the oxygen, microorganisms and infections can flourish the most in the circulatory system. Alkalizing is a need to kill the likelihood of sickness.

Diminishes aggravation: Over-acridity in the body can build irritation, when you have coronary illness, joint pain, or malignant growth your framework is in a fiery state. An eating regimen that comprises of alkaline-framing food varieties holds aggravation under wraps.

Reinforces Bone: As individuals age, the body normally goes through calcium from our bones Calcium in a vital factor in adjusting the blood and body pH. Without the calcium, our bones become weak, prompting osteoporosis.

What is an Alkaline Diet and how would I begin? An Alkaline eating routine permits us to put food varieties on a scale to characterize them as either corrosive shaping or alkaline-framing. By and large food sources with a pH level of 1-7 are considered acidic, or the meats, dairy and espresso we referenced before. Food varieties between 7-14 are considered alkaline and end up being supplement thick and cell reinforcement rich. Extraordinary instances of solid, alkaline food sources include: citrus organic products (esp. new lemon), vegetables and crude, natural nuts like almonds. Our's bodies will probably discover an equilibrium in the alkaline zone between 7.35 - 7.45 pH - to accomplish this a general guideline is to follow a 80/20 eating regimen with the goal that your day by day feast comprises principally of organic products and vegetables and less of meats and dairy (and espresso!).

1. Lamb dopiaza with broccoli rice

Prep:20 mins Cook:1 hr and 30 mins Serves 2

Ingredients:

- 225g sheep leg steaks , cut back of overabundance excess and cut into 2.5cm/1in pieces
- 50g full-fat characteristic bio yogurt , in addition to 4 tbsp to serve
- 1 tbsp medium curry powder
- 2 tsp cold-squeezed rapeseed oil
- 2 medium onions , 1 meagerly cut, 1 cut into 5 wedges

- 2 garlic cloves , stripped and finely cut
- 1 tbsp ginger , stripped and finely chopped
- 1 little red bean stew , finely chopped (deseeded in the event that you don't care for it excessively hot)
- 200g tomatoes , generally chopped
- 50g dried split red lentils , washed
- 1/2 little pack of coriander , generally chopped, in addition to extra to decorate
- 100g pack child leaf spinach
- For the broccoli rice
- 100g wholegrain brown rice
- 100g little broccoli florets

Technique:

1. Put the sheep in a large bowl and season well with ground dark pepper. Add the yogurt and 1/2 tbsp of the curry powder, and mix well to consolidate.

2. Heat a large portion of the oil in a large non-stick pot. Fry the onion wedges over a high heat for 4-5 mins or until gently browned and simply delicate. Tip onto a plate, put away and return the dish to the heat.

3. Add the excess oil, the cut onions, garlic, ginger and stew, cover and cook for 10 mins or until delicate, blending at times. Eliminate the top, increment the heat and cook for 2-3 mins more or until the onions are touched with brown – this will add loads of flavor, however ensure they don't get scorched.

4. Diminish the heat again and mix in the tomatoes and remaining curry powder. Cook for 1 min, at that point mix the sheep and yogurt into the skillet and cook over a medium-high heat for 4-5 mins, mixing routinely.

5. Empty 300ml virus water into the container, mix in the lentils and coriander, cover with a top and leave to cook over a low heat for 45 mins – the sauce ought to stew delicately and you can add a sprinkle of water if the curry gets somewhat dry. Eliminate the top each 10-15 mins and mix the curry.

6. With 30 minutes of the curry cooking time remaining, cook the rice in a lot of bubbling water for 25 mins or until simply delicate. Add the broccoli florets and cook for a further 3 mins. Channel well.

7. Eliminate the top from the curry, add the held onion wedges and keep on stewing over a high heat for a further 15 mins or until the sheep is delicate, blending consistently. Not long prior to serving, mix in the spinach, a modest bunch at a time, and let it shrivel. Present with the yogurt, coriander and broccoli rice.

Formula TIPS

Putting away LEFTOVERS

Freeze the cooked and cooled curry in sealable sacks or a cooler verification holder for as long as 2 months. Defrost for the time being in the cooler and reheat in a pan until steaming hot all through.

Works out positively For

Red pepper hummus with crispbread snaps

Yam dhal with curried vegetables

2. Lamb biryani

Prep:10 mins Cook:50 mins Plus at least 2 hrs marinating and resting Serves 6

Ingredients:

- 400g sheep neck, cut into little solid shapes
- 4 garlic cloves, ground
- 1 tbsp finely ground ginger
- 1 tbsp sunflower oil
- 1 large onion, chopped
- 1 tbsp cumin seeds
- 1 tbsp nigella seeds
- 1 tbsp Madras flavor paste
- 200g basmati rice, washed well
- 8 curry leaves
- 400ml great quality sheep or chicken stock

- 100g paneer, chopped
- 200g spinach, cooked and water pressed out
- To serve
- chopped coriander
- cut green chillies
- plain yogurt

Strategy:

1. Throw the sheep in a bowl with the garlic, ginger and a large touch of salt. Marinate in the cooler short-term or for at any a few hours.

2. Heat the oil in a meal. Fry the sheep for 5-10 mins until beginning to brown. Add the onion, cumin seeds and nigella seeds, and cook for 5 mins until beginning to mollify. Mix in the curry paste, at that point cook for 1 min more. Dissipate in the rice and curry leaves, at that point pour over the stock and bring to the bubble. Then, heat oven to 180C/160C fan/gas 4.

3. Mix in the paneer, spinach and some flavoring. Cover the dish with a tight top of foil, at that point put the top on to guarantee it's all

around fixed. Cook in the oven for 20 mins, at that point leave to stand, covered, for 10 mins. Carry the dish to the table, eliminate the top and foil, disperse with the coriander and chillies and present with yogurt as an afterthought.

3. Wild mushroom & ricotta rice with rosemary & thyme

Prep:10 mins Cook:45 mins Serves 2

Ingredients:

- 15g dried porcini mushrooms
- 1 tbsp balsamic vinegar
- 1 tbsp vegetable bouillon powder
- 1 tbsp rapeseed oil
- 1 large onion , finely chopped
- 200g pack little catch mushrooms
- 1 tbsp new thyme leaves
- 1 tsp chopped rosemary
- 3 garlic cloves , cut
- 170g brown basmati rice
- 2 leeks , washed and cut
- 50g ricotta

- 15g vegan Italian-style hard cheddar , finely ground
- parsley , to serve

Techniqu:

1. Put the dried mushrooms in an estimating container and pour over 800ml bubbling water. Mix in the balsamic and bouillon. Leave to drench.

2. Heat the oil in a large wok or griddle and fry the onion for 8 mins until delicate and brilliant. Add the catch mushrooms, thyme, rosemary, garlic and dark pepper, at that point cook, mixing at times, for 5 mins. Pour in the dried mushrooms and fluid, at that point mix in the rice and leeks.

3. Cover and leave to stew for 30 mins until the fluid has been ingested and the rice is delicate yet nutty. Eliminate from the heat, at that point mix in the ricotta and ground cheddar, and serve dissipated with parsley leaves.

4. Sticky chicken drumsticks & sesame rice salad

Prep:10 mins Cook:30 mins Serves 2

Ingredients:

- 4 chicken drumsticks
- 2 tbsp clear nectar , in addition to 1tsp
- 2 tbsp tamari (or soy sauce if not gluten free)
- 3 tbsp vegetable oil
- 2 tbsp sesame oil
- 120g basmati rice
- 70g kale , chopped
- juice 2 limes
- 100g radishes , divided
- 1 tbsp sesame seeds

Technique:

1. Heat oven to 200C/180C fan/gas 6. Put the drumsticks in a simmering tin. Blend 2 tbsp nectar, the tamari, 1 tbsp veg oil and 1 tbsp sesame oil in a bowl, at that point pour over the chicken – ensure each piece is covered. Cook for 25-30 mins.

2. Then, cover the rice with 240ml water and bring to the bubble. Cook for 8-10 mins until delicate. Back rub the kale with 1 tbsp veg oil for 5 mins until relaxing (this makes it less chewy). Sprinkle over the lime juice, remaining sesame oil and nectar, and season. Add the radishes and put away.

3. Fry the rice in the leftover veg oil in a non-stick container to dry out. Add to the kale, and throw to join.

4. Serve the drumsticks with the plate of mixed greens and dissipate over the sesame seeds.

Works out in a good way For

Minty summer rice salad

Crunchy green beans with radishes

Sesame barbecued asparagus pontoons

5. Thai broccoli rice

Prep:25 mins Cook:10 mins serves 4 (or 6 as a side)

Ingredients:

- 100g salted peanuts
- 1 head of broccoli , cut into florets and the stem cut down the middle
- 2 tbsp olive oil
- 1 red onion , finely diced
- 1 garlic clove , squashed
- 1 tbsp ground ginger
- 1 medium red stew , deseeded and finely diced
- ½ little red cabbage , shredded
- 1 red pepper , deseeded and cut into strips
- little pack coriander , generally chopped
- For the dressing

- zing and juice 1 lime
- 2 tbsp tamari
- ½ tbsp brilliant caster sugar
- 2 tbsp olive oil

Strategy:

1. Heat a skillet over a medium heat and add the peanuts. Toast equally, consistently shaking the dish, at that point eliminate and put away. Put the broccoli in a food processor and heartbeat until it would seem that green couscous grains. Void into a large bowl and put away.

2. Heat the oil in a large skillet and fry the onion, garlic, ginger and stew until delicate and fragrant. Add the broccoli rice to the skillet and blend through, ensuring everything is very much covered. Sauté for 3-4 mins until still somewhat firm. Move to a large bowl and add the red cabbage, red pepper, a large portion of the coriander and a large portion of the toasted peanuts. Blend to consolidate.

3. To make the dressing, whisk the lime zing and juice, tamari, sugar and oil together until

joined. Throw the dressing through the broccoli rice and move to a serving bowl or individual dishes. To serve, decorate with the leftover coriander and peanuts.

6. Smoky spiced Jollof rice & coconut-fried plantain

Prep:10 mins Cook:40 mins Serves 6

Ingredients:

- 400g basmati rice
- 400g can plum tomatoes
- 1 red pepper
- 1 red onion , divided
- 1 garlic clove
- 1 scotch cap bean stew (deseeded on the off chance that you don't care for it excessively hot)
- 4 tbsp vegetable oil or sunflower oil
- 3 straight leaves
- 1 thyme branch

- 1 tsp cayenne pepper
- 1 tsp smoked paprika
- 1 tsp ground cumin
- 1 tsp ground dark pepper
- 60g tomato purée
- For the singed plantain
- 4 tbsp coconut oil
- 2 plantains , stripped and cut into 1cm rounds

Technique:

1. Put the rice in a sifter, wash completely to eliminate the starch, at that point absorb clean virus water for 5 mins. Channel and standard heat up the rice for 5 mins until practically cooked, at that point channel, wash and put away.
2. Mix the tomatoes, pepper, a large portion of the red onion, the garlic and bean stew until smooth.
3. Finely cut the excess onion half. Heat the vegetable oil in a large, high-sided container. Add the cut onion, narrows and thyme, and cook on a medium heat for 8 mins until the onion is softened and sweet-smelling.

4. Add the flavors with 1 tsp ocean salt, cook for a couple of mins more, at that point add the tomato purée and cook for 1-2 mins.

5. Add a large portion of the tomato and pepper blend (freeze the rest for sometime later). Add the semi-cooked rice and blend completely to cover with the sauce. Add somewhat more water, turn down the heat, mix and cover with a top for 5-10 mins until cooked through. Cooking time will rely upon the kind of rice, so continue to check it. Try not to stress in the event that it gets on the base, this will add to the flavor. Season to taste and eliminate the cove leaves prior to serving.

6. To cook the plantain, basically heat the coconut oil in a high-sided container until hot. Fry the plantain, turning sometimes, for a couple of mins until delicate and brilliant. Present with the rice.

7. Roast cauliflower with prosciutto & taleggio

Prep:10 mins Cook:30 mins Serves 2-4

Ingredients:

- 1 large cauliflower
- olive oil , for brushing
- 125g taleggio cheddar , cut
- 4 cuts prosciutto
- 4 liberal tbsp crème fraîche
- 75g gruyère , ground
- rocket or watercress, delicately dressed, to serve (optional)

Strategy:

1. Heat oven to 220C/200C fan/gas 7. Eliminate the leaves from the cauliflower and cut out the base (without removing such a lot of that the head breakdowns). Slice the cauliflower down the middle, at that point into four cuts – two from every half – that are about 2cm thick. Put these on a heating sheet, brush done with oil and season with pepper (no salt). Cover the preparing sheet firmly with foil and cook for 12 mins.

2. Eliminate from the oven, remove the foil and turn the heat down to 200C/180C fan/gas 6. Set the sheet back and cook for 8 mins. Eliminate from the oven – the pieces ought to be brilliant on one side – and turn the cauliflower over. Put a portion of the taleggio, a cut of prosciutto and a spoonful of crème fraîche on every cauliflower piece. Sprinkle with the gruyère, at that point get back to the oven.

3. Cook for another 8 mins, or until the cauliflower is brilliant and the cheddar has dissolved. The cauliflower pieces ought to be totally delicate. Serve straight away with the

rocket or watercress, on the off chance that you like.

Works out positively For

Broccoli and cauliflower cheddar

Southern-style macintosh 'n' cheddar

Cauliflower steaks with broiled red pepper and olive salsa

8. Skinny lamb biriyani

Prep:15 mins Cook:20 mins Serves 2

Ingredients:

- For the cauliflower pilau
- 350g cauliflower florets
- ½ tsp turmeric
- 3 cardamom units , daintily squashed
- ½ tsp fennel seeds , daintily squashed
- a couple of portions of dark onion seeds or nigella seeds
- For the zesty sheep
- 1 tbsp rapeseed oil
- 1 large onion , finely chopped
- 1 tbsp finely chopped ginger
- 1 red bean stew , deseeded and finely chopped
- 2 garlic cloves , daintily cut

- 1 tsp ground cumin
- 1 tsp ground coriander
- 200g exceptionally lean sheep steak, cut into scaled down pieces
- 200g can chopped tomatoes
- 1 tsp bouillon
- 15g toasted chipped almonds
- 50g pomegranate seeds
- modest bunch little mint leaves

Technique:

1. Put the cauliflower in a food processor and heartbeat until it is diminished to rice-sized pieces. Tip into a large bowl and mix in the turmeric, cardamom, fennel seeds, dark onion seeds and some flavoring. Cover with stick film, puncture and put away.
2. For the zesty sheep, heat the oil in a non-stick wok and fry the onion and ginger for 10 mins until delicate and brilliant. Add the stew and garlic, and cook for 1 min more.
3. Mix in the cumin and coriander, cook momentarily, at that point throw in the sheep and pan fried food for 1-2 mins until pale

brown. Add the tomatoes and the bouillon, and cook for 2 mins - you are focusing on a thick sauce and truly delicate sheep that is still somewhat pink and delicious.

4. Then, put the cauliflower in the microwave and cook on high for 3 mins. Tip out onto serving plates, dab the sheep and sauce in patches over the rice, at that point dissipate with the almonds, pomegranate seeds and mint leaves to serve.

9. Lighter cauliflower cheese

Prep:20 mins Cook:30 mins Serves 4

Ingredients:

- 400ml semi-skimmed milk
- 2 tbsp cornflour
- 2 garlic cloves
- 1 large cauliflower , about 1kg, untrimmed
- 75g extra-develop cheddar , coarsely ground
- 25g parmesan , coarsely ground
- 1 tbsp clipped chives
- 1½ tsp Dijon mustard
- 150ml buttermilk

Technique:

1. Blend 2 tbsp of the milk with the cornflour and put away. Press the garlic cloves in a garlic smasher to crush – yet not pound – them. Put them in a container with the remainder of the milk and heat until simply going to the bubble. Quickly eliminate from the heat and leave to implant.

2. Trim any leaves from the cauliflower and cut out the thick principle tail, at that point cut the cauliflower into florets. Carry a large container of water to the bubble. Add the cauliflower, get back to the bubble, at that point stew for around 5 mins until just cooked yet with a touch of nibble.

3. Heat oven to 200C/180C fan/gas 6. Tip the cauliflower into a large colander, channel well, at that point move to a shallow ovenproof dish, about 1.5 liters (see tip, left). Combine the two cheeses as one. Mix 2 loaded tbsp with the chives and a pounding of pepper, and save for sprinkling over.

4. Mix the cornflour blend into the warm milk. Return the container to the heat and bring to the bubble, blending, until thickened and smooth. Eliminate from the heat, dispose of

the garlic, at that point mix in the cheddar until it has softened. Mix in the mustard and buttermilk, and season with pepper. Pour the sauce over the cauliflower to equally cover, at that point sprinkle over the held cheddar blend. Heat for around 25 mins or until rising round the sides and brilliant on top.

10. Vegan nuggets

Prep:20 mins Cook:40 mins plus 1 hr chilling

MAKES 30

Ingredients:

- 300g cauliflower florets (or 3/4 little cauliflower)
- 2 carrots , chopped (about 165g)
- ½ medium onion , chopped
- 1 tbsp olive oil
- 1 garlic clove , squashed
- 2 tbsp nourishing yeast
- 2 tsp yeast remove
- 400g can cannellini beans , depleted
- 50g gram (chickpea) flour
- olive oil , for the heating plate
- For the covering

- 100g gram flour , in addition to some extra
- 100g breadcrumbs (use sans gluten if vital)

Technique:

1. Heartbeat the cauliflower, carrots and onion in a food processor until finely chopped, similar to rice. Heat the oil in a large griddle and tenderly fry the blend for 12-15 mins until softened. Add the garlic and fry for a further 1 min, at that point remove the heat and mix in the healthful yeast and yeast extricate. Put away.

2. Mix the beans into a soft purée in a food processor, at that point add to the veggie blend and consolidate well. Mix in the flour and season. Put in the cooler to solidify for 1 hr.

3. Heat the oven to 220C/200C fan/gas 7. Line a large heating plate with preparing material and coat with a little olive oil. To make the covering, blend the gram flour with 150ml water using a fork so it takes after beaten egg, at that point season. Dissipate the additional gram flour on a plate and fill a second with the breadcrumbs.

4. Fold the bean combination into pecan estimated pieces, at that point smooth to frame chunk shapes. Dunk the pieces first in the gram flour, at that point in the gram hitter, lastly move in the breadcrumbs – handle cautiously as they will be somewhat delicate. At the point when the chunks are completely covered, spread them out on the readied plate.

5. Heat for 20 mins, at that point use utensils to turn every piece over and prepare for a further 15 mins until they are dim brilliant and fresh. Leave to cool for 20 mins prior to presenting with your decision of plunging sauces.

11. Courgette & cauliflower yellow curry

Prep:10 mins Cook:30 mins Serves 4

Ingredients:

- 2 tbsp vegetable oil
- 2 little onions , finely chopped
- 2 garlic cloves , squashed
- 2 tbsp yellow curry paste
- 400ml would coconut be able to drain
- 450g cauliflower florets
- 2 large courgettes , divided and cut
- 250g basmati rice
- 1 red bean stew , deseeded and cut
- little pack coriander , leaves as it were

Technique:

1. Heat the oil in a large, profound griddle and cook the onions for 5 mins until delicate, yet not browning. Add the squashed garlic and yellow curry paste and mix for a further 2 mins.

2. Pour in the coconut milk, add a large portion of a jar of water (using the coconut milk can), and bring to a delicate stew. When stewing, add the cauliflower and courgette. Cover and stew for 10 mins, at that point eliminate the top and keep cooking until the sauce decreases and thickens a bit. Season well.

3. Then, cook the rice adhering to pack directions. Serve in shallow dishes with the curry, finished off with the stew and a dissipating of coriander.

Works out positively For

Cauliflower rice

Coconut rice

Pea, feta and quinoa spring moves with broil tomato nam prik

12. Beef & lentil cottage pie with cauliflower & potato topping

Prep:20 mins Cook:1 hr and 20 mins Serves 4

Ingredients:

- 1 tbsp olive oil
- 250g minced meat
- 1 large carrot , coarsely ground
- 1 tbsp tomato purée
- 200g red lentil
- 600ml meat stock
- 140g frozen pea
- 1 ¼kg potato , cubed

- 1 large cauliflower (about 400g), cut into florets
- 150ml milk
- 50g spread
- 100g develop cheddar , ground

Strategy:

1. Heat oven to 200C/180C fan/gas 4. Heat the oil in a large dish and add the minced meat. Cook for 5 mins until browned all finished, at that point add the carrot and cook for 2 mins more.

2. Mix in the tomato purée and add preparing. Cook for a couple of mins, at that point add the lentils and stock. Stew for 20 mins, at that point mix in the peas.

3. In the interim, carry a container of water to the bubble and add the potatoes. Stew for 15 mins, at that point add the cauliflower and stew for a further 10 mins until the veg is delicate.

4. Channel, at that point return the veg to the search for gold few mins to dry out. add the milk, margarine and preparing, and pound

together. At last, add the cheddar, holding a modest bunch, and blend well. Cover and set to the side 500g of the squash blend for the frankfurter formula tomorrow (see 'works out positively for', right).

5. Spoon the mince into a large simmering dish, around 30 x 20cm, and spoon the squash over the top. Sprinkle with cheddar and heat until brilliant, around 30 mins.

13. Lentil lasagna

Prep:15 mins Cook:1 hr and 15 mins Serves 4

Ingredients:

- 1 tbsp olive oil
- 1 onion , chopped
- 1 carrot , chopped
- 1 celery stick, chopped
- 1 garlic clove , squashed
- 2 x 400g jars lentils , depleted, washed
- 1 tbsp cornflour
- 400g can chopped tomato
- 1 tsp mushroom ketchup
- 1 tsp chopped oregano (or 1 tsp dried)
- 1 tsp vegetable stock powder
- 2 cauliflower heads, broken into florets
- 2 tbsp unsweetened soya milk

- touch of newly ground nutmeg
- 9 dried without egg lasagne sheets

Strategy:

1. Heat the oil in a container, add the onion, carrot and celery, and tenderly cook for 10-15 mins until delicate. Add the garlic, cook for a couple of mins, at that point mix in the lentils and cornflour.

2. Add the tomatoes in addition to a canful of water, the mushroom ketchup, oregano, stock powder and some flavoring. Stew for 15 mins, mixing every so often.

3. In the interim, cook the cauliflower in a dish of bubbling water for 10 mins or until delicate. Channel, at that point purée with the soya milk using a hand blender or food processor. Season well and add the nutmeg.

4. Heat oven to 180C/160C fan/gas 4. Spread 33% of the lentil blend over the foundation of an earthenware preparing dish, around 20 x 30cm. Cover with a solitary layer of lasagne, snapping the sheets to fit. Add another third of the lentil blend, at that point spread 33% of

the cauliflower purée on top, trailed by a layer of pasta. Top with the last third of lentils and lasagna, trailed by the leftover purée.

5. Cover freely with thwart and prepare for 35-45 mins, eliminating the foil for the last 10 mins of cooking.

14. Marinated lamb leg, romanesco & pickled walnuts

Prep:30 minsCook:30 minsplus overnight marinating Serves 6

Ingredients:

- 1.2kg sheep back end or boneless leg, parceled into equivalent pieces
- 500g live normal yogurt
- little pack rosemary , leaves and stalks isolated
- 2 entire romanesco , leaves eliminated
- 3 tbsp vegetable oil
- 7 salted pecans , 4 finely chopped and 3 split for serving, in addition to 1 tbsp pickling fluid
- 60ml olive oil

- 500ml new sheep stock

Strategy:

1. The prior night, cut back the excess from the sheep at that point blend in with the yogurt and rosemary leaves. Cover and put in the ice chest to marinate for the time being.

2. The following day, trim the tail off a romanesco so it sits upstanding on a board. Cut 5cm off each side with a bread blade (keep these off-slices to make the couscous). Cut the remainder of the romanesco into three thick cuts. Rehash with the other romanesco. Oil a large, non-leave preparing plate with 1 tbsp vegetable oil. Lay the romanesco cuts in a solitary layer and sprinkle with somewhat more vegetable oil. Season with salt and dissipate over the rosemary stalks, prepared to broil.

3. Finely slash or heartbeat the romanesco off-cuts in a food processor until they are the surface of couscous. Blend the finely chopped pecans into the couscous with the olive oil, and season with salt.

4. Heat oven to 200C/180C fan/gas 6. Wipe the marinade off the sheep and season with ocean salt. Heat 2 tbsp vegetable oil a large ovenproof skillet. Fry the sheep until brilliant all finished, at that point broil in the oven for 8-12 mins, contingent upon how uncommon you like it. Put the romanesco in the oven simultaneously. When the sheep is prepared, eliminate from the oven, flip the romanesco cuts over so they roast on the two sides, and cook for a further 10 mins. Cover and rest the sheep in the search for gold mins.
5. In the interim, stew the stock in a wide pan with 1 tbsp of the pecan pickling vinegar from the container for 10 mins until it frames a jus.
6. Cut the sheep and present with the romanesco cuts, some couscous, a large portion of a pecan and the jus.

15. Cauliflower & cheese fritters with warm pepper relish

Prep:30 mins Cook:1 hr and 20 mins Serves 5

Ingredients:

- For the squanders
- 1 cauliflower - you need 350g/12oz
- 100 g/4 oz plain flour
- 4 eggs , beaten
- 100 g/4 oz feta cheddar , generally disintegrated into little lumps
- 125g ball mozzarella , attacked little pieces
- zing 1 lemon , in addition to wedges to serve
- little pack level leaf parsley , generally chopped
- olive oil , for fricasseeing
- For the relish

- 1 onion , chopped
- 2 red peppers , chopped
- little piece ginger , finely ground
- 2 garlic cloves , squashed
- 1 red stew , chopped (leave the seeds in)
- 1 tbsp olive oil
- 2 tsp yellow mustard seed
- 250 g/9 oz tomatoes , generally chopped assuming large, left entire if cherry
- 50 g/2 oz delicate light brown sugar
- 50 ml/2 fl oz red wine vinegar
- 2 tbsp sultana

Strategy:

1. For the relish, mellow the onion, peppers, ginger, garlic and stew in the oil in a large pot. Once softened, add the mustard seeds, tomatoes, sugar and vinegar. Cover and stew for 30 mins, at that point uncover and stew for 10 mins more until delicate and tacky as opposed to excessively sassy. Mood killer the heat and mix in the sultanas. This relish will keep in the refrigerator for as long as 3 days, or freeze for as long as a month.

2. Heat up a large pot of water. Quarter the cauliflower and remove the majority of the focal large tail. Weigh 350g cauliflower for the formula and put the rest in the cooler to utilize some other time. Generally cleave the cauliflower – you should wind up with a blend of little florets and some better pieces. When the water is bubbling, add all the cauliflower, cover and cook for 3 mins precisely. Promptly channel, at that point tip everything back into the pan and set back over a low heat, to dry out for a couple of mins.

3. Put the flour into a large bowl with a lot of preparing and bit by bit race in the eggs to make a smooth hitter. Mix in the cheeses, lemon zing and the majority of the parsley, at that point tenderly mix in the entirety of the cauliflower.

4. Pop your oven on low so you can keep the wastes warm while you cook in clusters. Spot an old tough oven plate (anything unstable may clasp) or a durable skillet or iron straight onto the grill. Wipe with some olive oil, at that point spoon on some combination to make approximately 10-12cm round wastes. Fry for

3-5 mins until brilliant under and the player simply looks set on the top, at that point utilize a fish cut to flip the squanders over and push down with the rear of the cut to crush any large cauliflower bits and smooth the bottoms a piece. Cook again for 3-5 mins until brilliant, at that point move to a material lined plate and keep warm in the oven while you cook the rest.

5. To serve, warm up the relish somewhat, disperse the squanders with outstanding parsley and add some lemon wedges.

Works out in a good way For

Grilled sheep with sweet mint dressing

16. Charred spring onion & olive rice salad

Prep:15 mins Cook:15 mins Serves 8 as a side

Ingredients:

- 100g pitted Spanish green olives , depleted
- bundle spring onions (150g)
- 1 tsp olive oil
- 750g cooked blended grains and rice (or 3 x 250g pockets)
- 3 tbsp sherry or red wine vinegar
- 100g sundried tomatoes , cut
- 50g chipped almonds , toasted
- 2 celery sticks, chopped
- 50g manchego shavings or vegan elective (optional)

Technique:

1. String the olives onto metal or bamboo sticks. Heat an iron container or light the grill, at that point when the flares have subsided and the coals are white, throw the spring onions with the oil and barbecue for 8-10 mins to cook until delicate. Barbecue the olives for a couple of mins, turning routinely, until they look somewhat singed. Eliminate the spring onions from the barbecue and cut into reduced down pieces. Eliminate the olive sticks from the flame broil.

2. Heat the grains and rice pockets, if using, in the microwave for 2 mins until warm. Throw with the vinegar, some flavoring and the sundried tomatoes with a little sprinkle of the oil from the container. Leave for a couple of mins for the dressing to be retained.

3. Throw the olives, spring onions, toasted almonds and celery into the rice. To serve, mix through the manchego, if using, and season to taste.

Formula TIPS

COOKING WITH OLIVES

Burning olives makes them juicier just as giving incredible surface and profundity of flavor.

KEEP IT VEGAN

To guarantee the plate of mixed greens is veggie lover, use juice vinegar (or check the mark on the red wine or sherry vinegar), preclude the manchego and top with extra chipped almonds or entire toasted almonds, generally chopped. You can likewise add 4 tbsp raisins, for pleasantness, on the off chance that you like.

17. Jerk chicken with rice & peas

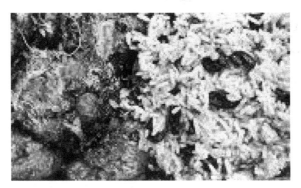

Prep:25 mins Cook:45 mins

Plusovernightmarinating Serves 6

Ingredients:

- 12 chicken thighs, bone in
- 1 lime, divided
- hot sauce, to serve (optional)
- For the marinade
- 1 major bundle spring onions, generally chopped
- thumb-sized piece ginger, generally chopped
- 3 garlic cloves
- ½ a little onion
- 3 scotch cap chillies, deseeded in the event that you need less heat
- ½ tsp dried thyme, or 1 tbsp thyme leaves
- 1 lime, squeezed

- 2 tbsp soy sauce
- 2 tbsp vegetable oil
- 3 tbsp brown sugar
- 1 tbsp ground allspice
- For the rice and peas
- 200g basmati rice
- 400g would coconut be able to drain
- 1 bundle spring onions, cut
- 2 large thyme branches
- 2 garlic cloves, finely chopped
- 1 tsp ground allspice
- 2 x 410g jars kidney beans, depleted

Technique:

1. To make the jerk marinade, consolidate the spring onions, ginger, garlic, onion, scotch hat chillies, dried thyme, lime juice, soy sauce, vegetable oil, brown sugar and ground allspice in a food processor alongside 1 tsp salt, and mix to a purée. In case you're experiencing difficulty getting it to mix, simply continue killing the blender, mixing the combination, and attempting once more. At last it will begin

to mix up – don't be enticed to add water, as you need a thick paste.

2. Taste the jerk combination for preparing – it should taste pretty pungent, however not terribly, puckering pungent. You would now be able to toss in more chillies if it's not zesty enough for you. On the off chance that it tastes excessively pungent and harsh, have a go at including a touch more brown sugar until the combination tastes even.

3. Make a couple of cuts in 12 chicken thighs and pour the marinade over the meat, scouring it into every one of the hole. Cover and leave to marinate for the time being in the ice chest.

4. On the off chance that you need to grill your chicken, get the coals consuming 1 hr or so before you're prepared to cook. Valid snapped meats are not by and large flame broiled as we consider barbecuing, however kind of smoke-barbecued. To get a more valid jerk insight, add some wood chips to your grill, and cook your chicken over lethargic, circuitous heat for 30 mins.

5. To cook in the oven, heat to 180C/160C fan/gas 4. Put the chicken pieces in a broiling

tin with the divided lime and cook for 45 mins until delicate and cooked through.

6. While the chicken is cooking, set up the rice and peas. Wash the basmati rice in a lot of cold water, at that point tip it into a large pot. Add the coconut milk, spring onions, thyme twigs, garlic and ground allspice.

7. Season with salt, add 300ml virus water and set over a high heat. When the rice starts to bubble, turn it down to a medium heat, cover and cook for 10 mins. Add the kidney beans to the rice, at that point cover with a top. Leave off the heat for 5 mins until all the fluid is ingested.

8. Crush the broiled lime over the chicken and present with the rice and peas, and some hot sauce on the off chance that you like it truly hot.

18. Chicken mole with coriander rice

Prep:30 mins Cook:2 hrs Serves 6

Ingredients:

- 2 ancho chillies
- 2 tbsp sunflower oil
- 8 bone-in chicken thighs , skins eliminated
- 2 onions , chopped
- 2 tsp ground cumin
- 1 ½ tsp cinnamon
- 3 garlic cloves , generally chopped
- 50g raisin
- 2 tbsp smooth peanut butter
- 2 tbsp chipotle paste

- 400g can chopped tomato
- 25g dim chocolate (search for one with at any rate 70% cocoa solids)
- 1 little red onion , cut into rings
- juice 1 lime , in addition to wedges to serve (optional)
- 150ml pot soured cream
- For the coriander rice
- 600g long grain rice
- large pack coriander , finely chopped
- zing 2 limes and squeeze of 1

Technique:

1. Put the chillies in a bowl and add sufficient bubbling water to simply cover. Leave to mellow for 20 mins. In the event that you can't discover anchos, flame broil red peppers until they're truly darkened and delicate. Cool them, at that point strip and use depending on the situation in the formula, adding 1 tsp smoked paprika and some additional chipotle to re-make the sweet, smoky flavor.

2. In the interim, heat the oil in a flameproof meal dish, season the chicken, at that point

brown on all sides. You may need to do this in bunches so you don't stuff the dish. Eliminate to a plate. Add the onions to the dish and cook for 5 mins until softened. Add the flavors and cook for 1 min until fragrant.

3. Eliminate the chillies from their splashing fluid, holding the fluid, and dispose of the stalks and seeds. Put in a food processor with 4 tbsp of the drenching fluid, the garlic and raisins. Whizz to a paste, at that point tip into the dish. Add the peanut butter, chipotle paste, tomatoes and 400ml water (top off the tomato can and twirl to get all the tomato bits out). Return the chicken to the dish and season. Cover with a top and stew, blending sporadically, for 1 hr.

4. Eliminate the chicken pieces to a plate. Using 2 forks, shred the meat and dispose of the bones. Return the chicken to the sauce, add the chocolate and keep cooking, revealed, for 30 mins more. In the event that the sauce resembles it's getting excessively thick, add a portion of the bean stew dousing fluid or some water.

5. Cook the rice adhering to pack guidelines. In the interim, put the red onion in a little bowl. Add the lime juice and a touch of salt. Leave to pickle until prepared to serve. At the point when the rice is cooked, add the coriander and lime zing and squeeze, and cushion up with a fork. Eliminate the mole from the heat, disperse with the salted red onion and serve close by the rice, with soured cream and lime wedges, in the event that you like.

Formula TIPS

Stew KNOW-HOW

Ancho is the name given to the dried poblano pepper, which is filled in South America and utilized in its dried structure to season sauces and stews. Ancho chillies are large, with dim brown or dark skins and a sweet, raisin-like flavor. They have a medium zest.

19. Beef rendang & turmeric rice

Prep:40 mins Cook:2 hrs and 30 mins Serves 6

Ingredients:

- 3 tbsp vegetable oil
- 2kg hamburger shin or skirt, cut into reduced down 3D shapes
- 2 lemongrass stalks, slammed (see 'Tip' for how to plan)
- 2 x 400ml jars coconut milk
- 4 tbsp parched coconut
- 2 kaffir lime leaves, torn
- 1 ½ tbsp chicken stock powder (we utilized one from an Asian general store)
- 2 tbsp tamarind paste
- 1 tsp brilliant caster sugar
- ¼ tsp salt

- For the paste
- 15 dry chillies
- 6-8 child shallots
- thumb-sized piece ginger, chopped
- thumb-sized piece galangal, stripped and chopped (utilize ginger in the event that you can't discover it)
- 3 lemongrass stalks, chopped
- For the rice
- 2 tbsp oil
- 2 tsp mustard seeds
- 2 tsp turmeric
- 10 curry leaves (optional)
- 700g jasmine rice
- 2 tsp chicken stock powder

Technique:

1. For the paste, absorb the chillies bubbling water for 15 mins. Channel, eliminate seeds and whizz with the remainder of the paste ingredients in a little food processor until smooth.

2. Heat the oil in a wok or a weighty based flameproof goulash dish. Fry the paste for 5

mins until the fragrance is delivered. Add the meat and the lemongrass, and blend well. When the hamburger begins to lose its pinkness, add the coconut milk and 250ml water. Bring to the bubble, at that point lower to a stew, uncovered. Mix infrequently to abstain from staying, and all the more frequently towards the end.

3. In the mean time, toast the coconut in a griddle on a low heat for 5-7 mins until brilliant brown. Put away to cool. Using a blender, coarsely mix it to better pieces – yet not very fine. Put aside.

4. After 2 hrs, add the coconut, kaffir lime leaves, chicken stock powder, tamarind paste, sugar and salt to the container. Stew for 30 mins more. You should begin to see the oil isolating from the blend. It's prepared when the meat is delicate and practically self-destructing.

5. For the rice, utilize a substantial based pot with a cover. Heat the oil in the dish and add the mustard seeds. When the seeds begin popping, add the turmeric, curry leaves (if using) and rice, and blend well. Add the chicken stock and 1 liter of water. Bring to the bubble, at that

point go down to the least stew and cook, covered, for 5 mins. Eliminate from the heat, with the cover on and leave to steam for 25 mins.

Formula TIPS

Planning LEMONGRASS

Strip off the main layer and utilize the base, less sinewy part just, disposing of the top 5cm. Any extras freeze well.

20. Pollo en pepitoria

Prep:35 mins Cook:1 hr and 10 mins Serves 4

Ingredients:

- great touch of saffron
- 4 tbsp additional virgin olive oil
- 6 garlic cloves
- 35g whitened almonds
- 30g flat bread , torn
- 2 tbsp parsley , chopped, in addition to extra to serve
- 8 skin-on and bone-in chicken thighs
- 1 onion , finely chopped
- 1 carrot , chopped
- 1 celery stick, chopped
- 250ml dry sherry

- 350ml chicken stock
- 1 cinnamon stick , broken in two
- touch of ground cloves
- 2 sound leaves
- 2 eggs , hard-bubbled, shelled and split
- 2 tbsp chipped almonds , toasted

Strategy:

1. Put the saffron in a little bowl with 75ml of just-bubbled water. Mix and put away. Heat 2 tbsp of the oil in an expansive, shallow goulash dish. Cook the garlic until pale gold in shading, at that point add the whitened almonds and bread, and keep on singing until everything is brilliant. Tip into a food processor with some salt and pepper and the parsley, and whizz together.

2. Heat 2 more tbsp of the oil in the container and brown the chicken all finished, preparing as you cook. Put in a bowl and put away.

3. Eliminate everything except around 2 tbsp of chicken fat from the container and cook the onion, carrot and celery until brilliant. Add the sherry, blending to remove any brown pieces

that have adhered to the skillet. Pour in the stock and the saffron (with its water), and bring to the bubble, at that point turn the heat down to a stew. Add the flavors and straight leaves, and set the chicken back in the skillet with any juices. Season and tenderly cook the chicken for around 40 mins with the top on.

4. Move the chicken to a bowl once more, leaving the sauce in the skillet, and cover with foil to keep warm. Eliminate the yolks from the eggs and generally slash the whites. Pound the egg yolks in a little bowl and continuously blend a few tbsp of the sauce. Carry the leftover sauce to the bubble to decrease a messed with (you need it to simply cover the chicken), at that point turn the heat down. Eliminate the inlet and cinnamon stick. Add the egg yolks and cook for a couple of mins until the blend has thickened. Mix in the almond combination that you made before (this will thicken the sauce, as well). Set the chicken back in the container and heat it for around 3 mins, spooning the sauce over it. Season to taste.

5. Disperse over the additional parsley, the almonds pieces and the chopped egg whites (in

case you will utilize them). You can serve this directly from the dish with some rice, in the event that you like.

21. Spicy nduja arancini

Prep:35 mins Cook:1 hr Makes 20

Ingredients:

- 2 tbsp olive oil
- 1/2 onion, finely chopped
- 1 large garlic clove, squashed
- 1/2 tsp fennel seeds, squashed
- 300g risotto rice
- 400g can chopped tomatoes
- 800ml hot chicken stock
- 80g parmesan, finely ground
- 50g nduja hotdog, finely chopped
- 150g mozzarella, cut into 3D shapes
- 100g plain flour
- 3 medium eggs, beaten
- 200g panko breadcrumbs

- vegetable oil, for profound searing

Strategy:

1. Heat the olive oil in a goulash dish over a low heat, and fry the onion with a touch of salt for 10-12 mins, or until softened. Add the garlic and fennel seeds, and cook for 1 min more. Mix in the rice and cook

2. Pour in the tomatoes and a large portion of the stock, and turn the heat to medium-high. Cook, mixing persistently, until the stock is totally vanished. Add the excess stock, a spoon at a time, adding more when the past option is consumed by the rice. Cook until the rice is still somewhat firm, around 15-20 mins.

3. Mix in the parmesan and nduja, at that point spread the risotto out over a preparing plate and leave to cool to room temperature.

4. Scoop the cooled risotto into 20 even segments, marginally larger than a golf ball. Smooth one of the balls into a circle in your grasp, put a piece of mozzarella in the middle, at that point encase with the rice. Fold into a

ball. Rehash with the leftover risotto and mozzarella.

5. Tip the flour, eggs and panko breadcrumbs into three separate shallow dishes. Roll every risotto ball in the flour, at that point the egg, lastly the breadcrumbs. Move the balls to a heating plate. Half-fill a large, hefty based pot with vegetable oil and heat over a medium-low heat to 170C, or until a slice of bread becomes brilliant in the oil inside 45 seconds. Cautiously lower the risotto balls into the oil in clumps, and fry each bunch for 8-10 mins, or until brilliant brown and gooey in the middle. Channel on a plate fixed with kitchen paper.

Formula tip

To freeze, make the formula up to the furthest limit of stage 3, at that point pack the risotto balls into a large food sack and freeze. Thaw out altogether in the ice chest short-term before profound fricasseeing.

22.   Creamy tomato risotto

Prep:5 mins Cook:35 mins Serves 4

Ingredients:

- 400g can chopped tomato
- 1l vegetable stock
- handle of spread
- 1 tbsp olive oil
- 1 onion, finely chopped
- 2 garlic cloves, finely chopped
- 1 rosemary twig, finely chopped
- 250g risotto rice
- 300g cherry tomato, split
- little pack basil, generally torn
- 4 tbsp ground parmesan

Technique:

1. Tip the chopped tomatoes and a large portion of the stock into a food processor and heartbeat until smooth. Fill a pan with the excess stock, bring to a delicate stew and keep over a low heat.

2. Then, place the margarine and oil in the foundation of a large pan and heat delicately until the spread has dissolved. Add the onion and delicately cook for 6-8 mins until softened. Mix in the garlic and rosemary, at that point cook for 1 min more. Add the rice and cook, blending, for 1 min.

3. Begin adding the hot stock and tomato combination about a quarter at a time. Allow the risotto to cook, blending regularly, adding more stock as it is retained. After you have added a large portion of the stock, add the cherry tomatoes. After 20-25 mins, the rice ought to be smooth and delicate, the cherry tomatoes softened and the entirety of the stock ought to be spent.

4. Cover and leave for 1 min, at that point mix in the basil. Serve sprinkled with Parmesan and a decent pounding of dark pepper.

23. Arancini balls

Prep:40 mins Cook:1 hr and 5 mins Makes 18

Ingredients:
- 2 tbsp olive oil
- 15g unsalted margarine
- 1 onion, finely chopped
- 1 large garlic clove, squashed
- 350g risotto rice
- 150ml dry white wine
- 1.2l hot chicken or veg stock
- 150g parmesan, finely ground
- 1 lemon, finely zested
- 150g ball mozzarella, chopped into 18 little pieces
- vegetable oil, for profound searing
- For the covering
- 150g plain flour
- 3 large eggs, softly beaten
- 150g fine dried breadcrumbs (panko functions admirably)

Technique:

1. Heat the oil and margarine in a pan until frothy. Add the onion and a touch of salt and fry tenderly over a low heat for 15 mins, or until softened and clear. Add the garlic and cook for another min. Mix in the rice and cook for a further min, at that point pour in the wine. Bring to the bubble and cook until the fluid is diminished significantly. Pour into equal parts the stock and stew, blending ceaselessly, until the vast majority of the fluid is retained. Add the leftover stock a ladleful at a time as the rice ingests the fluid, blending, until the rice is cooked through (this should take around 20-25 mins). Mix in the parmesan and lemon and season to taste. Spread the risotto out into a lipped plate and leave to cool to room temperature.

2. Scoop the cooled risotto into 18 equivalent segments – they ought to be somewhat larger than a golf ball. Level a risotto ball in your grasp and put a piece of the mozzarella in the middle, at that point encase the cheddar in the rice and fold it into a ball. Rehash with the leftover risotto balls.

3. Put the flour, eggs and breadcrumbs into three separate shallow dishes. Dunk each readied risotto ball into the flour, trailed by the eggs lastly, the breadcrumbs. Move to a plate and put away.

4. Half-fill a large, hefty based pot with vegetable oil and heat over medium-low until it peruses 170C on a cooking thermometer or until a slice of bread becomes brilliant brown in the oil

inside 45 seconds. Lower the risotto balls into the oil in clusters and cook for 8-10 mins, or until brilliant brown and softened in the middle. Put away on a plate fixed with a spotless kitchen towel.

5. Eat the arancini warm, or present with a fundamental pureed tomatoes for plunging.

Formula TIPS

ROLLING THE ARANCINI

Utilize somewhat wet hands to fold the risotto into balls – this will help shape the arancini, and stay away from any dilemmas.

24. Fragrant pork & rice one-pot

Prep:15 mins Cook:30 mins Serves 4

Ingredients:

- 4-6 great quality hotdogs
- 1 tbsp olive oil
- ½ onion , finely chopped
- 2 garlic cloves , squashed
- 2 tsp each ground cumin and coriander
- 140g long grain rice
- 850ml vegetable stock
- 400g can chopped tomato
- ½ little pack coriander , leaves picked

Strategy:

1. Split the hotdog skins, press out the meat, at that point fold it into little meatballs about the size of a large olive. Heat the oil in a large non-stick pan, at that point brown the meatballs well on all sides until cooked – you

may have to do this in clumps. Put the meatballs away.

2. Add the onion and garlic to the container. Relax for 5 mins, mix in the flavors and rice, at that point cook for another min. Pour in the stock and tomatoes. Bring to a stew, scraping up any sausagey bits from the lower part of the skillet. Stew for 10 mins until the rice is simply cooked, at that point mix in the meatballs with some flavoring. Scoop into bowls, dissipate with coriander and present with dry bread.

Formula TIPS

TIP

The most straightforward approach to roll a meatball is with somewhat wet hands – it will stop the blend adhering to your fingers.

MAKE IT WITH PASTA

Italian pork balls with spaghetti: Brown the frankfurter meatballs in a griddle until brilliant, at that point put away. Relax the onion and garlic as above, at that point mix in 1 tsp dried oregano, the chopped tomatoes, ½ can water and 1 tsp sugar. Stew until sassy, at that point mix in the meatballs for a couple of mins until cooked through. Serve over spaghetti, finished off with ground Parmesan.

Works out in a good way For

Caramel apple disintegrate

25. Tamarind aubergine with black rice, mint & feta

Prep:25 mins Cook:40 mins Serves 4

Ingredients:
- 2 large aubergines
- 4 tsp tamarind paste
- 2 tsp sesame oil
- 1 red stew , deseeded and daintily cut
- 1 tbsp sesame seeds
- 200g dark rice
- 6 spring onions , finely cut
- 100g feta , disintegrated
- 2 little packs mint , generally chopped
- little pack coriander , generally chopped, holding a couple of leaves, to serve
- zing 1 large lime
- For the dressing
- 2 tbsp dull soy sauce
- juice 1 lime

- 5cm/2in piece ginger , stripped and finely ground (juices what not)
- touch of sugar

Strategy:
1. Heat oven to 200C/180C fan/gas 6. Slice the aubergines down the middle lengthways and, with the tip of a blade, score the tissue profoundly in a mismatch precious stone example – however don't penetrate the skin. Push on the edges of the parts to open the cuts. In a little bowl, consolidate the tamarind paste and sesame oil. Brush the combination over the aubergine, driving it into the cuts. Spot on a heating plate, sprinkle over the bean stew and sesame seeds, at that point broil, cut-side up, for 25-35 mins or until the tissue is truly delicate.
2. Put the rice in a little strainer and wash under running water for 1 min until the water runs clear. Tip the rice into a little pan and add 650ml virus water. Bring to the bubble, decrease the heat and stew for around 35 mins until the rice is delicate. Channel under chilly running water.
3. Make the dressing by whisking every one of the ingredients along with a spot of salt. Change the flavoring to taste, adding somewhat more sugar, salt or lime juice, in the event that you like.
4. In a major bowl, combine as one the dark rice, spring onions, feta, mint, chopped coriander, and the lime zing and dressing. Sprinkle the

saved coriander leaves over the aubergine parts and present with the rice.

26. Mauritian chicken curry

Prep:20 mins Cook:30 mins Serves 4

Ingredients:

- 2 tbsp vegetable oil
- 8 curry leaves , finely chopped
- 1 medium onion , finely chopped
- 2 garlic cloves , finely ground
- 2cm ginger , finely ground
- 1 cinnamon stick
- 1 green stew , finely chopped
- 1 tbsp thyme leaves
- 3 tbsp Mauritian curry powder
- 600g skinless chicken thigh filets, chopped
- 2 medium tomatoes , chopped
- 2 large potatoes , cut into quarters
- ½ red onion , finely cut, to serve
- 1 tbsp coriander leaves , to serve
- basmati rice , cut cucumber, new rotis and satini pomme d'amour, to serve
- For the satini pomme d'amour
- 2 large ready tomatoes , finely chopped

- 1 green stew , finely chopped
- ½ white onion , finely chopped
- 1 tbsp olive oil

Strategy:

1. Heat the oil in a large pot over a low-medium heat. Drop in the curry leaves, onion, garlic, ginger, cinnamon stick, stew and thyme and cook for 5 mins until the onion has softened, mixing routinely to forestall adhering to the skillet.
2. Blend the curry powder with a sprinkle of water in a bowl to make a runny paste. Add the paste to the dish and give it a decent mix until fragrant, around 30 seconds. Keeping the heat on a low-medium stew with the goal that the flavors don't consume, add the chicken pieces and mix to cover in the curry.
3. Add the chopped tomatoes, potatoes and 1 tsp salt. Pour in water to simply underneath the level of the chicken and potatoes. Cook for around 25 mins until the potatoes and chicken are cooked through, at that point dispose of the cinnamon stick.
4. To make the satini pomme d'amour, combine every one of the ingredients as one in a bowl. Spoon the curry into bowls and dissipate over the coriander leaves and red onion. Present with fleecy basmati rice, cucumber cuts, rotis and the satini pomme d'amour.

Conclusion

Thank you for picking this book. This book contains recipes which are more healthful and based on alkaline diet. These contain eggs, fruit, vegetables and meat. A body that follows an alkaline diet may benefit from a variety of healthy advantages. So try to prepare at home and enjoy.

CPSIA information can be obtained
at www.ICGtesting.com
Printed in the USA
BVHW092105240621
610373BV00002B/304

.